D1559425

QUESTIONS JESUS ASKED

Visit our web site at
WWW.ALBAHOUSE.ORG

or call 1-800-343-2522 (ALBA)
and request current catalog

Questions Jesus Asked

Provisions for the Spiritual Journey

JOEL GIALLANZA, CSC

ST PAULS

Alba
House

Library of Congress Cataloging-in-Publication Data

Giallanza, Joel.
    Questions Jesus asked : provisions for the spiritual journey /
Joel Giallanza.
    p. cm.
    ISBN: 0-8189-0924-2 (alk. paper)
    1. Spiritual life—Christianity.   I. Title.

    BV4501.3.G53 2002
    242'.5— dc21   2002018688

Produced and designed in the United States of America by the
Fathers and Brothers of the Society of St. Paul,
2187 Victory Boulevard, Staten Island, New York 10314-6603,
as part of their communications apostolate.

ISBN: 0-8189-0924-2

Printing Information:

Current Printing - first digit   1   2   3   4   5   6   7   8   9   10

Year of Current Printing - first year shown

2002   2003   2004   2005   2006   2007   2008   2009   2010

Dedication

To my parents
who taught me to listen
for the questions

Table of Contents

QUESTIONS JESUS ASKED

"I Will Also Ask You a Question"

"May I ask a question?" "I believe we have to vote, I call the question." "This will not be an easy question to address." "I question the truth of that assertion." These are simple, everyday statements. And precisely because expressions like these can be so commonplace, we may overlook their significance. One aspect of our uniqueness as human beings lies in our capacity to ask a question. We cleverly assign this ability, anthropomorphically, to everything from pets to a variety of inanimate objects. Nevertheless, it is a distinctive characteristic of human life that we can pose a question in all its forms.

The term *question* is quite versatile in itself, having at least four meanings. First, it refers to a statement that invites or calls for a reply; it is the simple act of making an inquiry. Second, a question can refer to some point under discussion; we are accustomed to this meaning in more formal settings where parliamentary procedure is used to call for a vote. Third, the term refers to a difficult or controversial matter to be resolved; we examine and analyze the matter, working to discover a solution. Fourth, it refers to an uncertainty about the topic under consideration; we may doubt the truth or accuracy of a statement or the interpretation of an event. Depending upon the rich nuances within a specific language or culture, there may be even more meanings.

The thread weaving all these meanings together is rooted in the etymology of the word. The most ancient meaning of *question* is "to seek." A question then, at least by inference, is associated with the terms "search" and "quest." Our ability to question, in whichever form it emerges, reflects that we are on a quest, we are searching, we are looking for information or insight.

This is a particularly intriguing etymology when viewed from the perspective of our faith. The quest becomes much more than the pursuit of information, though that may be part of our need and intention at the moment. In the light of faith, a question is part of the search for truth. It is an exploration into that truth that will make a difference in our life. We discover that we are seeking God. Our questions can provide energy and direction for our search, and the quality of our questions can hasten or hinder that search.

This human characteristic, this ability to ask a question, is reflected in the way we make and maintain our relationship with the Lord. Many prayer forms, both personal and communal, both within and without Christianity, are petitions in which we ask for a favor or assistance or insight. The spirituality underlying this form of prayer is simple and significant. Through petitions we bring our needs before God; we learn that we are dependent upon God and able to trust God. By our petitions, we practice that dependence and trust.

There is a persuasive and powerful influence generated by those dimensions of contemporary culture which equate any sort of dependence with weakness. The logic which Saint Paul learned from the Lord — "whenever I am weak, then I am strong" (2 Corinthians 12:10) — would be nonsense by many of our standards. Nevertheless, faith teaches us that we are indeed strongest when we call upon the Lord, when we depend upon the Lord, when we are "weak" enough to bring a question, a petition, to the Lord. The alternative is pride which always creates distance between ourselves and the Lord.

Those cultural traits which tend to counteract the essential dependence on the Lord necessary for a healthy and whole spiritual life can gradually persuade us to believe that we are self-contained. We become convinced that all the resources we would need — possibly even for salvation — are within us. Gradually, we neglect and forget to turn to the Lord with our needs and, eventually, the quest itself is no longer a priority in our life. We will have no more questions for the Lord because we will insist that we have an ample supply of our own ready answers.

"Where Are You?"

What are the roots of this human capability to ask a question? We must reach back to our creation itself to discover an answer. We read in the book of Genesis, "God said, 'Let us make human-kind in our image, according to our likeness'" (1:26). Our human abilities reflect the capacities of God who created us. And the God who created us is a God of questions. We are in relationship with and loved by a God who questions.

A God with questions is searching. "The man and his wife heard the sound of the Lord God walking in the garden at the time of the evening breeze, and the man and his wife hid themselves from the presence of the Lord God among the trees of the garden. But the Lord God called… 'Where are you?'" (Genesis 3:8-9). This is the first of God's questions. "Where are you?" There are many other questions which God places before humanity during the course of salvation history. But the significance of this first question marks God as one who searches, as one who is on a quest, for us. God is seeking us even as we seek God; we seek precisely because we are being sought. The goal of the spiritual life is to bring together the paths of our search and of God's search. The goal of the quest is that we be one with God.

"I will also ask you a question" (Luke 20:3). It is not surprising, then, to discover Jesus as a person whose life and ministry are filled with questions. Even a quick glance through the gospels is sufficient to see that questions are a regular part of Jesus' presence and activity, his message and ministry. There are questions from Jesus, "Why does this generation ask for a sign?" (Mark 8:12). There are questions to Jesus, "Why do you speak to them in parables?" (Matthew 13:10). And there are questions about Jesus, "Who is this who even forgives sins?" (Luke 7:49). The nature of these questions ranges from a basic search for information about a situation or event, "Where are we to buy bread for these people to eat?" (John 6:5), to a confrontation which challenges those who are called upon to answer, "Why do you call me 'Lord, Lord,' and do not do what I tell you?" (Luke 6:46). Sometimes the tone is comforting, "Woman, has no one condemned you?" (John 8:10); and sometimes it is quite unsettling, "How can you escape being sentenced to hell?" (Matthew 23:33). Whatever the nature of the question, though, it can give us some further insight into the person and mission of Jesus, and so support us along the pathways of our journey.

Spirituality of the Question

These present reflections are based on seven key questions from Jesus. The chapters are designed to be reflective and meditative, not exegetical. Their purpose is to provide a resource for nurturing our spiritual life and enhancing our relationship with the Lord. They present the foundations for a spirituality of the question, a spirituality which is single-minded in seeking the Lord. What can our ability to question teach us about the spiritual life?

First, it is within human nature to question. And because our nature reflects the image and likeness of God, our ability to question tells us something of God's nature. Indeed, we can identify a multitude of questions from God within both the Hebrew and the Christian Scriptures. A God of questions is a living God, an interactive God, a God with whom we can relate along the paths of our spiritual journey. A God with questions is a God about whom we can never presume to know everything, a God from whom there is always something to learn, a God of surprises.

Second, our ability to question reflects a desire to know, to probe, to seek the truths that lie beyond the limits of the self. Asking a question, in whichever form or tone, indicates some level of willingness to go beyond one's own world. Or, by the question, we invite someone else to consider a perspective beyond their own limited horizons. Those who will not consider looking beyond the boundaries of their present knowledge and experience tend not to ask questions precisely because they may have to deal with the new vistas that open in response to the question.

Third, questions place us on a journey to discover and uncover whatever or whomever we are seeking. They express our willingness to move into unfamiliar and even unknown territory, to look, to learn. They reflect a desire to grow, to develop, to expand. Questions are at least one indication that we are alive, that we have not yet reached the full capacity of our life. Those who have no questions have frozen their life as it is. Without an openness to new information, new light, new perspective, our energy for the journey diminishes, our desire to explore gradually dies, and our journey staggers or stops altogether.

The questions which are used here must be addressed from the perspective of our personal experience, as a means of strengthening our relationship with the Lord and of guiding our journey to the Lord. They are provisions for that relationship and that journey. Purely academic or theoretical responses may provide some information useful for our journey. But that information can also remain far removed from the practices of our everyday life unless we identify and implement the connections that need to be made.

Jesus' questions are personal and pastoral. They touch the actual situation or condition of his listeners. On those occasions when his questions appear to be academic or even adversarial, they have emerged in response to the narrow-minded parameters upon which others have insisted. Even then, however, the 'shock value' of his questions has a pastoral dimension insofar as it invites the intended respondent to consider a broader perspective or an alternate interpretation.

Our responses to these questions from Jesus must come from the heart of our personal experience. Otherwise, they will not reflect our identity, our faith, and our hope. And, to the degree that they do not reflect the truth of our experience, to that degree our responses are not authentic. They will not mirror the full richness of the God in whose image and likeness we are created. They will not lead us to be ever more people of love.

Setting Out on This Journey

As a simple preparation for this meditative journey with Jesus' questions, it may be helpful to reflect on how his questions affect us as individuals. Recall those questions from the gospels with which you are most familiar and ask yourself: Which questions do I find affirming and comforting? Which questions are challenging and even unsettling to me? Such reflection can give us some preliminary insights into those areas of life which yet need to be addressed for our continued growth and development. It may also indicate to us ways in which the Lord is calling us toward further progress.

"I will also ask you a question." May these reflections accompany us on a journey which brings us ever closer to the Lord. And yet, as always, it will be the Lord who guides us, giving us the courage we need to look ever deeper into the truth and beauty of our creation in God's own image and likeness. Then we, too, can affirm and strengthen one another with a question, "Were not our hearts burning within us while he was talking to us on the road?" (Luke 24:32).

"Who Do You Say That I Am?"

> When Jesus came into the district of Caesarea Philippi, he asked his disciples, "Who do people say that the Son of Man is?" And they said, "Some say John the Baptist, but others Elijah, and still others Jeremiah or one of the prophets." He said to them, "But who do you say that I am?" (Matthew 16:13-15)

People had opinions about Jesus and there were, no doubt, a wide range of stories floating around about him and his associates. And, as with any public figure, some of those stories may have been far removed from reality. Jesus must have been aware of this and he must have realized that the disciples would have been exposed to and even asked about the content of those stories. Logically, then, he inquires about what they may have heard, "Who do people say that the Son of Man is?"

The disciples recount what they have heard among the people. That could have been the end of the discussion. However, Jesus inquires further, probing to a much more personal level; "But who do you say that I am?" We can imagine the disciples falling silent in the face of such a blunt and probably unexpected question. It is one matter to report what others are saying; it is a completely different matter to articulate what one personally believes in response to Jesus. The question remains urgently relevant in our own times. If we claim to be followers of Jesus of Nazareth, then we will and must confront this question. It is the question of FAITH and it is directed to each of us. Who do I say Jesus is? What does Jesus mean in my life? How would my life be different without Jesus?

We can formulate a response to Jesus' question by reflecting on what faith calls us to do. What are the characteristics of a living faith? In living our faith we demonstrate, by our example, our response to Jesus' probing and personal question, "Who do you say that I am?" The opening verses of Saint John's first letter provide a framework for examining the quality of our faith.

> We declare to you what was from the beginning, what we have heard, what we have seen with our eyes, what we have looked at and touched with our hands, concerning the word of life — this life was revealed, and we have seen it and testify to it, and declare to you

the eternal life that was with the Father and was revealed to us — we declare to you what we have seen and heard so that you also may have fellowship with us; and truly our fellowship is with the Father and with his Son, Jesus Christ. (1:1-4)

Among the most intriguing attributes of this text is its references to the senses: "heard," "seen with our eyes," "looked at and touched with our hands." We can experience the Lord within and around us; we can sense the Lord's presence and activity. Faith is a gift from God rooted in our experiences of the Lord. However subtle those experiences may be, they lead us to a conviction and a choice which proclaim that Jesus of Nazareth is Lord. Jesus thus becomes the central priority in our everyday life. Whatever other realities may contribute to the formation of our identity, our personal experience of Jesus remains primary among them. While we do not share the same historical and physical proximity to Jesus as did Saint John, the heart of this experience remains the same: a personal acknowledgment and acceptance of Jesus as Lord.

It is particularly interesting to note that John refers to "what we have heard" first of all. In fact, hearing does have a connection to the development of our faith. In the Hebrew Scriptures, the Old

Testament, God's self-revelation is usually communicated through the spoken word. "Thus says the Lord," "Hear the word of the Lord," "Listen, my people," are regular refrains throughout the Old Testament. Admittedly, there are also visions through which God is revealed, but they are not as numerous as the occasions when God speaks to the people through the words of the prophets or other leaders.

In the Christian Scriptures, the New Testament, Saint Paul writes in his letter to the Romans, "Faith comes from what is heard, and what is heard comes through the word of Christ" (10:17). And, at the beginning of Saint John's gospel, Jesus' very identity is synonymous with the Word. "In the beginning was the Word, and the Word was with God, and the Word was God" (1:1). The Word must be spoken if it is to be heard. If Jesus is not preached, then the invitation to faith is never extended. As Saint Paul says of the people, "How are they to call on one in whom they have not believed? And how are they to believe in one of whom they have never heard? And how are they to hear without someone to proclaim him?" (Romans 10:14). The Word calls us to live our faith. What, then, are the characteristics of a living faith?

Faith Reaches Out to Others

Faith is not self-enclosed; it impels us to reach beyond ourselves, to touch the lives of others, to make a difference in our world. Saint John writes, "We declare to you what was from the beginning, what we have heard, what we have seen with our eyes, what we have looked at and touched with our hands, concerning the word of life." Faith is not designed to be a prized and private personal possession, stored away for safekeeping. Faith that is not declared and lived is no faith at all. The basis of ministry and of the various kinds of service within the church is precisely the living faith which communicates the Lord's message and continues the Lord's mission.

The message cannot preach itself and the mission cannot progress of itself. Jesus has commissioned his followers to bear the responsibility for that preaching and progress. Our gifts and skills and talents are the means through which we reach out to others, serve them, and so continue the work which the Lord has initiated and now has given us to do. Like faith, our gifts, skills, and talents are meant for service. While we can and will benefit personally from them in a variety of ways, if we do not share them, then their potential for good gradually diminishes.

Significant among those gifts, skills and talents are our experiences of the Lord, our personal relationship with the Lord. Faith is never a theory, it is alive and must be practiced to remain a living reality. As Saint James reminds us, "faith by itself, if it has no works, is dead" (2:17). Faith becomes most apparent when it is put into action. Our lives as followers of Jesus cannot be invisible, they must be working models of everyday faith for others to see. In this way we support and accompany others in their life of faith. Our daily life as a working model of following Jesus will speak most clearly to others if it is built upon the personal relationship we have made and now maintain with the Lord. Our support and accompaniment must be extended from the truth and strength of our own experiences. Theoretical models may provide some basic information, but only a living model is worthy of imitation.

Living faith reaches out to others. It must; indeed, it is among the greatest means we have for inviting others to follow Jesus. If faith remains hidden, then we become witnesses only to its diminishment. If we do not share faith, then it suffocates. Living faith and sharing faith can transform our world, person by person, beginning with ourselves.

Faith Gathers Us Into Community

Faith is not self-enclosed, nor is it self-sufficient; it places us in relationships with others. Even more, faith is the foundation for Christian community, it gathers us into community, and it marks us as community. Saint John writes, "We declare to you what we have seen and heard so that you also may have fellowship with us." In reaching out to others we extend the invitation for them to be united with us in following the Lord. The bond of faith weaves us together as God's own people, the church. Together we become a means for the transformation of our world.

The very nature and mission of the church involves reaching out and inviting in; its purpose is to preach the message and promote the mission of Jesus by faith. As a Christian community, we are gathered in faith. So essential is this identifying element, that apart from its foundation in faith, the church could be characterized as a humanitarian organization. It would do good works and provide valuable services in response to needs, but it would not thereby automatically communicate Jesus' message and continue his mission. By faith the church is a community; specifically, it is the community of God's people. And as a people brought together in faith, we are mandated to witness to the life, death, and resurrection of Jesus.

As a people of faith we are also a people of

hope. We proclaim that the promises of the Lord are true and to be trusted. We announce that God will not abandon us and that God's presence and activity remain constant in our world. We are people with hope to bring wherever we go in this broken world, a world unsure about the shape of its future, and a world that sometimes wonders if there will be a future. Faith and hope distinguish us as a community of love. We remain united by our love for one another and for all in response to God's love for us. "We love because God first loved us" (1 John 4:19). God's presence and activity among us are ever marked by love. As we remain in that love we become living witnesses of God's care and compassion for our world, healing its brokenness and building its future in faith and with hope.

Living faith gathers us into community. Faith is not self-nurturing; it supports others and seeks support from others. There is a natural mutuality about faith. It does not isolate and insulate itself from those we meet along the pathways of our spiritual journey. Quite the contrary, it desires their company. Faith is transmitted in community and nourished by community. Together we discover and fulfill the Lord's will for us, together we witness to God's work among us.

Faith Calls Us to Prayer

Faith is an explicit relationship with the Lord. It reaches out to others and gathers us into community; but, above all, it roots our life in God. Saint John writes, "Truly our fellowship is with the Father and with his Son, Jesus Christ." Faith calls us to prayer because this is a primary means of nourishing our relationship with the Lord. If we desire to discover and fulfill God's will for us, if we want to witness to God's work around us, then we must be people of prayer. We must be willing to invest time and energy into this relationship. And, as with any relationship, if we do not attend to it, then it will die or at least diminish in value for us.

How we invest that time and energy is not as significant as that we actually designate the time and energy to be invested. Fidelity is ever the priority. Yet even with this priority, prayer must have some real form. Otherwise it becomes little more than a pious thought with no practical application. The rich mystical tradition of the church is replete with a wide spectrum of prayer forms, reflecting the diverse array of human personalities and the many ways in which individuals throughout history have expressed their relationship with God and their longing for God. So ample is the spectrum of prayer forms that it is almost necessary to use some descriptive adjective before the term *prayer* so the meaning is clear in spoken or written words.

It is beyond the scope of these present reflections to explore a multitude of prayer forms. The emphasis here is that we recognize prayer, in all its forms, as an indispensable channel through which we can remain sensitive to the Lord's presence and activity in our life and our world. Without a personal discipline of prayer, and a commitment of fidelity to it, our Christian life gradually loses touch with the very faith which reaches out to others and gathers us into community. Eventually, we can become oblivious to God's word and work within and around us.

Living faith calls us to prayer. If we believe, then we pray. Our fidelity to prayer is one gauge of the priority we have assigned to our relationship with the Lord. We can say anything we want about the importance of the Lord in our life. The truth of that importance is found, not in the eloquence of our words, but in the effectiveness of our work in remaining faithful to prayer. Any relationship needs regular contact between those involved if it is to remain alive. There is no difference in our relationship with the Lord; without regular contact through prayer, it will begin to deteriorate. And with that deterioration, the value we place on reaching out to others and on gathering as community will gradually decay.

"Who Do You Say That I Am?"

This is the question of faith. Our response to this question proclaims the priority of the Lord Jesus in our life. The caliber of our response will become evident most clearly in our everyday life, through our ordinary tasks and responsibilities. Within our daily life we will either confirm or contradict our commitment to reach out to others through sharing and service, to gather with and contribute to the faith community in worship and mutual support, and to pray. Every day we are challenged to demonstrate the quality of our response to Jesus' question. The task before us is to take up the challenge and to live our response.

"Do You Know What I Have Done to You?"

> After Jesus had washed the disciples'
> feet, had put on his robe, and had re-
> turned to the table, he said to the dis-
> ciples, "Do you know what I have done
> to you?" (John 13:12)

This brief text appears in the scene tradition-
ally referred to as the "Last Supper." The festive
meal shared by Jesus and his disciples is situated
not long before all the activities surrounding the
Passion of Jesus begin to unfold. At this point in
his gospel, Saint John notes that Jesus "knew that
his hour had come to depart from this world"
(13:1). It is time for Jesus to bid farewell to his
disciples; what he does, then, during this meal is
particularly significant.

Jesus' action during the course of this meal
must have been culturally shocking to the disciples.
Here is the "Teacher and Lord" (13:13) doing the
unimaginable, washing feet; a task usually assigned
to household servants in first-century Jewish cul-

ture. However much the disciples may have lacked in the refinements of household etiquette, even they would have taken note of this unexpected activity on the part of their leader. There must have been some squirming among the disciples as Jesus quietly went about this humble chore of hospitality. Except for Peter's protest, "You will never wash my feet" (John 13:6), there is relative silence. We know, of course, that Jesus prevailed even with Peter, and so completed the task.

After all this Jesus asks the question that opened these reflections, "Do you know what I have done to you?" There are at least two levels on which we can interpret this question. First is the obvious level of the immediate context. Jesus has just washed the disciples' feet, and in doing so has given them an example to be followed, a model of service that is to mark their relationships with one another and with all people. A second level is much broader. Jesus' question can also extend far beyond this immediate context to include everything that the disciples had experienced with Jesus since the beginning of their association with him. So much had transpired since their first encounter with Jesus. They have received and come to know so many things. Now they are called to share what they have received and what they know.

In our own relationship with Jesus we, too, receive and learn; we, too, are called to share. This is the question of GIFTS. Do I know what the

Lord has done to me? What are my gifts? Do I use those gifts? We can begin to shape our response to Jesus by reflecting on the nature of the gifts we have received and on the means by which we receive them. By knowing and using our gifts we can live our response to Jesus' question, "Do you know what I have done to you?" A text from Saint Paul's first letter to the Corinthians provides a basis for exploring the nature of gifts.

> There are varieties of gifts, but the same Spirit; there are varieties of services, but the same Lord; and there are varieties of activities, but it is the same God who activates all of them in everyone. To each is given the manifestation of the Spirit for the common good. (12:4-7, 11)

This text presents the gifts we receive from the perspectives of diversity and unity. In terms of diversity, Saint Paul reminds us "there are varieties of gifts... services... activities." The gifts we receive from God are not mere copies of one another; there is a genuine diversity among them. They have different forms and functions. Everyone does not receive exactly the same gifts. In terms of unity, at work within these diverse gifts, it is "the same Spirit... Lord... God." The gifts are many, but their unifying principle is ever the same, our triune God. Gifts draw us into union with one another. As diverse as our gifts may be within the faith community, they do not create divisions among us. We create our own divisions by neglecting the Lord in our midst. The faithful use of gifts fashions us into the Body of Christ. We become one even as Jesus prayed that "they may be one, just as we are one" (John 17:22).

The last sentence in this text from Saint Paul will serve as the lens through which we will look at the nature of the gifts we have received. "To each is given the manifestation of the Spirit for the common good."

Gifts Are Given to Each Individual

There are at least two points which can be drawn from the first part of this sentence; both points are beneficial for arriving at a deeper understanding of the nature of gifts.

First, since gifts are given to each individual, every person is gifted by God. Gifts do not divide us into categories of those who have and those who do not have. No one can claim to have no gifts from God. However, it is possible that we might not recognize our individual gifts or know what to name them. I may not perceive that I am patient in frustrating situations or generous with my time or compassionate to those who are struggling, yet others will experience that patience, generosity, and compassion. The gifts are there; and once they are recognized, they must be exercised. Our gifts mature and develop through use; they are not designed to be kept in safe storage and preserved untouched. If they are so restricted, they will show more mold than maturity when we do attempt to use them.

Our gifts can become moldy, but they will not be missing. God's gifts to each individual are irrevocable. Gifts are an expression of God's love for us and God's presence and activity within us. Throughout salvation history, that love, presence, and activity have not waned. This truth is articulated eloquently by the prophet Isaiah. "I have called you by name, you are mine. Because you are precious in my sight, and honored, and I love you, I give people in return for you, nations in exchange for your life. Do not fear, for I am with you!" (43:1, 4-5). Jesus himself reiterated these encouraging words, "I am with you always, to the end of the age" (Matthew 28:20). This same truth applies to gifts: God does not take back what has been given. We have the option of using, not using, or misusing those gifts. Our gifts are responsibilities, not decorative additives to our personality. Once we acknowledge and accept them, we bear the responsibility to use them.

Second, the gifts that are given to each individual are personalized. Gifts are not given in the same way that paint is sprayed on an object. Even the same gift will be expressed differently from one person to another. There is no generic expression for the gifts of patience, kindness, gentleness, listening, understanding, generosity, compassion, or any other of the gifts which God lavishes upon us. Individual personalities and the specific circumstances to which the person is responding will shape the expression of the particular gift being used. Because they are personalized, gifts are adaptable precisely so we can respond appropriately and effectively to the different situations we encounter.

The significance of this personalization is the exclusion of comparison or competition with one another. No one gift is necessarily greater or more powerful than another. The single exception is clearly articulated by Saint Paul, "the greatest of these is love" (1 Corinthians 13:13). Love is the gift which encompasses all the others simply because it reflects fully the example and standard established by Jesus for his followers. Even more, as Saint John teaches us, "God is love" (1 John 4:8). The number of gifts we have is no criterion for holiness; only our likeness to the Lord Jesus can serve as such a measure. Our gifts remind us of the extravagance of God's mercy and generosity, they teach us of God's power at work in and through us, they proclaim God's love for us. Gifts can reveal to us the beauty of ourselves and of each person, a beauty rooted firmly in our creation in God's own image and likeness.

Gifts Are the Manifestation of the Spirit

Where there are gifts, there is the Spirit of God. Our gifts are not self-generated, they are grounded solidly in God who is the source of them all. We cannot feign God's gifts — at least not for very long. We will consume a great deal of time and energy trying to maintain an attitude, a stance, a behavior that necessarily relies on the support of God's gifts to us. Pretense is always spiritually expensive and exhausting. Eventually, our efforts will collapse, as will our stamina for generating the appearance of having one or another gift. Feigning a gift is an exercise in pride; it is arrogance before God and a deception before the people. It draws attention to the self for some momentary honors of being perceived as holy. However, in situations where the gift may be truly needed, the feigning falters and betrays our spiritual theatrics. Feigned gifts ultimately point to the self and spotlight the self. Genuine gifts always point to the Lord.

Where there are gifts, there is the Spirit of God. Our gifts are not self-sustained; they flow from grace and flourish by grace. God's gifts are irrevocable, but if we do not maintain an active relationship with God through personal prayer and participation in the faith community, we can begin to take our gifts for granted. Misuse then becomes a distinct possibility. We will gradually lose respect for the sacredness of the gift and regard for the greatness of its source. Then our awareness of the gifts and our attentiveness to their true purpose begin to erode. God alone can sustain our gifts; our task is to seek that sustenance.

Our God is an incarnational God. Jesus came among us, to be with us and to give us an example of living in union with God. Jesus embraced the life of humanity that we might embrace the life of God. Thus, through our humanity and through our encounters with others we manifest the life of God we have embraced. Jesus taught us that we would be recognized as his followers by the quality of our relationships; specifically, by our love for one another. It is no different with any of God's gifts; all of them are meant to be visible. That is their incarnation, that is a manifestation of the Spirit. The mission and message of Jesus continue through our use of the gifts we have received.

Our gifts, what the Lord has done to us, reflect the work of the Spirit in our life and in our world. Where there are gifts from God, there is the Spirit of God. Our awareness and acknowledgment of the gifts which God has lavished upon us are a lesson in humility. Our use of those gifts, rather than isolating us from God, teach us an ever greater dependence on God and a keener understanding that God is the source of our gifts and the strength of our power to do good. The Lord has given us gifts so our everyday life can become a manifestation of the Spirit, so the quality of our relationships will demonstrate once again for all to see that "the Word became flesh and lived among us" (John 1:14).

Gifts Are Given for the Common Good

"To each is given the manifestation of the Spirit for the common good." Our gifts are given primarily for others; this is precisely why they are meant to be visible, so others in need can call upon us to use our gifts. We can surely derive some benefit from our gifts, but that is not their primary purpose. Always, they are for the common good. Gifts are relational by nature; through them we are in relationships with others and by them we are at the service of others. A gift that could be self-contained is no gift at all; for such confinement, such inability to extend itself, would significantly diminish its visibility and seriously drain its vitality for building up the Body of Christ. As our faith reaches out to others, so our gifts serve others. If we do not use those gifts for others, then we compromise their purpose.

Gifts are not self-proclaimed. They are made visible and become known through our relationships with others. How do we truly know that we are gifted with patience or kindness, gentleness or compassion, listening or understanding, or any one of the multitude of God's gifts? Our gifts are verified by others, not by our proclamation of them. Other people, based on their experiences of relating to us, will confirm or contradict the truth of our gifts. They will know and see our gifts at work, sometimes even before we are fully aware of those gifts ourselves. We need only recall an instance in which someone told us we possessed a particular gift that we had not yet fully recognized within ourselves. Their comment to us may have been the lens through which we were able to see new ways in which God had gifted us.

Gifts, like holiness itself, must be evident to others. We can say anything we want about the quality of a specific gift that is ours, but that statement must be consistent with our behaviors and our attitudes. True gifts are always much more than mere words; they form an intricate weaving with our everyday activities. They are not limited to special appearances, but rather become a part of our usual routine. Gifts shape the way we respond to whomever we encounter, in any situation. By God's grace, our gifts become natural to us.

If the gifts that we claim to have are truly ours, then we use them for the good of others instinctively, without needing to ponder and plan our response. Even more, we are not alone in this. As we use our gifts for the good of others, so too, they will use their gifts for us. Such is the rich and interactive diversity within the Body of Christ, the church. This diversity is for mutuality, not division. The gifts are many, yet we are called to be one in the Lord. Our focus remains ever on the Lord within us and around us. Together, as followers of Jesus, we witness to the full richness of the Spirit's presence and activity in our church and in our world. And there is no greater witness our gifts can present.

"Do You Know What I Have Done to You?"

This is the question of gifts. Our response to this question challenges us to recognize the gifts we do have and to acknowledge God as the source and sustenance of those gifts. As we grow and mature along the pathways of our spiritual journey, so too will our gifts. The more we come to know, understand, and use our gifts, the sharper will be our perspective on the gifts which others have received. We come to believe that each person is gifted, each person is called to be a manifestation of the Spirit for the common good. We answer Jesus' question by discovering and developing our gifts. We demonstrate that answer through the quality and integrity of our daily life.

"Do You Want to Be Made Well?"

In Jerusalem by the Sheep Gate there is a pool, called in Hebrew Bethzatha, which has five porticos. In these lay invalids — blind, lame, and paralyzed. One man was there who had been ill for thirty-eight years. When Jesus saw him lying there and knew he had been there a long time, he said to him, "Do you want to be made well?" (John 5:2-6)

Tradition held that an angel of God would periodically stir the water in the pool; further, the first one to enter the water during that time would be healed of whatever the affliction. This is the background for the man's response to Jesus' question. "Sir, I have no one to put me into the pool when the water is stirred up; and while I am making my way, someone else steps down ahead of me" (John 5:7). Jesus does not respond to the man's explanation with a discussion of the possible logistics for assuring that he could be the first one placed in the pool the next time; rather, Jesus speaks a word of healing. And so it is. "At once the man was made well" (John 5:9).

From one perspective it could be said that Jesus was asking about the man's desire, and yet the man focused only on the difficulty. Admittedly, the man's concern about the practical difficulties he has encountered in the past is, by implication, an affirmative response to Jesus' question. Nevertheless, if Jesus had not acted apart from the logic of what the tradition said about the procedure to be followed, the man would have remained sitting helplessly by the water, possibly for the rest of his life. As it is, though, Jesus asks the question of HEALING and a different scenario unfolds.

We, too, are confronted with this question in a variety of ways. Through our faith and with the gifts we have received, we can experience and have confidence in the goodness and graciousness of God. In the light of that faith and those gifts we can also experience and know our own weakness, our capacity for alienation from God, and our need to rely on God. Thus we come to recognize those dimensions of our life which long for and need the healing touch of God.

In responding to Jesus' question, it is important that we know ourselves and are aware of those dimensions in our life which need healing. And we should know something about healing itself so our expectations are realistic without being restrictive.

A familiar text from the letter of James will provide the framework for these reflections on healing.

> Are any among you sick? They should call for the elders of the church and have them pray over them, anointing them with oil in the name of the Lord. The prayer of faith will save the sick, and the Lord will raise them up; and anyone who has committed sins will be forgiven. Therefore confess your sins to one another, and pray for one another, so that you may be healed. The prayer of the righteous is powerful and effective. (5:14-16)

This text from Saint James cannot be reduced to a recipe; it is much more a call to trust in God's presence and power at work in and through the faith community. It is also a challenge to compassion and sensitivity for one another, and a call to recognize the significance of mutual prayer. What does this important text teach us about healing?

Healing is a Gift to the Community

In reading through the gospels and the Acts of the Apostles we recognize that healing was a regular part of Jesus' ministry. So too it was a regu-

lar part of the work by which the disciples continued the mission of Jesus. However, relatively
quickly in Christian history, healing began to be
viewed as specialized and extraordinary. Its regu-
larity was not so evident. Some Christians even
came to believe that praying for a healing disrupted
the way in which God's will was meant to unfold
in a person's life, and so they discouraged such
prayer. Healing appeared to have lost its status as
a usual gift of the Spirit, regularly given and used
for continuing Jesus' mission. Yet, what Saint Paul
has said about the gifts given to God's people
stands firm. "To one is given through the Spirit
the utterance of wisdom, and to another the utterance of knowledge according to the same Spirit,
to another faith by the same Spirit, to another gifts
of healing by the one Spirit" (1 Corinthians 12:8-
9). Healing remains a gift given to and within the
Christian community.

Healing is multifaceted. It reflects the richness and diversity of all those in the Christian community. Too often healing is spoken about as if its
extent is limited almost exclusively to the physical
dimension of our life. As significant as that is for
us, we know by experience that there are other dimensions of our life which need the touch of God's
healing power. Our emotional and affective life,
our relationships and our spiritual life can be disrupted by a variety of past and present issues which
affect them. Those disruptions, if left unaddressed,

can seriously compromise our quality of life. They must be transformed by healing. Saint Paul writes of this gift in the plural, indicating that it is limited neither to one form nor to one dimension of our life. "God has appointed in the church first apostles, second prophets, third teachers; then deeds of power, then gifts of healing, forms of assistance, forms of leadership, various kinds of tongues" (1 Corinthians 12:28). Thus, we can speak of emotional and relational, spiritual and psychological — as well as physical — healing.

The channels through which we can be touched by the gift of healing are equally diverse. We can constrict our openness to the gift of healing if we assume that it is communicated through a very limited number of channels. Healing assuredly can come through prayer but, in conjunction with that prayer, it may reach us by way of medical doctors and counselors, spiritual directors and friends, relatives and others who accompany us along the paths of our spiritual journey. Healing can also reach us through our own reading and reflection, our discernment and discovery. The challenge is not to question whether God can heal, but to determine the most appropriate and effective channel for responding to the specific need for healing in our life. If we believe this gift is an expression of God's power, then we need only seek the way in which the healing will come.

Healing is a gift to the community, unfolds

within the community, and is shared by the community. In speaking to those who are ill, Saint James first recommends that they "call for the elders of the church." The presence and support of others can be and often is a powerful channel through which we receive healing. We call upon the "elders," that is, those whose wisdom and experience can assist us in identifying what needs to be healed, confronting it, and taking whatever steps are needed to facilitate the healing we seek from the Lord.

Healing Calls Us to Faith and Prayer

Do we believe in God's power to heal? It is simple enough to give an affirmative response to this question on an academic or idealistic level. But when we consider our particular situation at the moment, our response may be much less certain. We might not be prone to "call for the elders" — in whichever form that takes for our situation — because we feel nothing would be accomplished. Faith opens us to the possibility of God's healing power. Admittedly, we do not control that power by faith, but apart from faith it may never even occur to us that we can ask for healing. We then relegate healing to an archival collection of quaint and ancient stories that no longer touch contemporary daily life. Healing calls us to faith.

If we believe, then we pray. As healing calls us to faith, so it calls us to prayer. In writing about those who are ill, Saint James relates that the elders will "pray over them, anointing them with oil in the name of the Lord." As we stand in need of healing, we must pray, we must recognize our need for others' prayer, and then we must be willing to have others pray for us. As healing calls us to prayer, so it calls us to the humility and honesty which enable us to ask for prayer, to recognize our need for prayer, and to accept our responsibility to pray. The alternative is a pride which becomes impenetrable, and so opportunities for inviting God's healing into our life pass us by. Healing calls us to prayer.

Faith and prayer are truly inseparable; they are so intertwined with one another that each supports and strengthens the other. Saint James tells us that "the prayer of the righteous is powerful and effective." The power and efficacy of that prayer are founded firmly on faith, on the conviction that God is intimately involved in our everyday life. Nevertheless, the faith and prayer to which healing calls us are not guarantees of certainty; rather, they are marks of hope. Saint Paul reminds us, "in hope we were saved. Now hope that is seen is not hope. For who hopes for what is seen? But if we hope for what we do not see, we wait for it with patience" (Romans 8:24-25). So it is with healing; we believe, we pray, we hope.

Healing calls us to faith and prayer. It remains for us to determine if we will respond, if we will open ourselves to the Lord who can touch and transform any dimension of our life. Through faith and prayer we confirm our response and cultivate our openness to the Lord. Saint James assures us, "the prayer of faith will save… will raise them up." Through our faith and prayer we await and welcome the Lord's word and work of healing within us.

Healing is the Lord's Work

Healing is a gift to the community and it does call us to faith and prayer, but healing ever remains the work of the Lord. Saint James is clear in telling us that the anointing is done "in the name of the Lord" and that "the Lord will raise up" those who are ill. In praying for the Lord's gifts and in using the Lord's gifts for the good of others, our focus must remain fixed on the Lord who is the origin of those gifts. While this truth applies to every gift we receive, it is particularly applicable to healing so we do not forget that the source and sustenance of the power to heal are not centered in ourselves.

If we distort or lose our perspective on the truth that healing is the Lord's work, then we can live with the delusion of thinking that healing is a self-generated personal possession which functions according to our whims. In the Acts of the Apostles we read of a Samaritan magician, named Simon, who was renowned for his skills, "saying that he was someone great" (8:9). He had witnessed the works of the apostles and especially that "the Spirit was given through the laying on of the apostles' hands" (8:18). Wanting to have this power, he offers a bribe to Peter and John. Peter's response is uncompromising. "May your silver perish with you, because you thought you could obtain God's gift with money! You have no part or share in this, for your heart is not right before God" (8:20-21). Healing is the Lord's work; it cannot be purchased or possessed, proffered or practiced, according to our preferences and priorities.

We do not control God's gifts, but we can not be completely passive in regard to them either. Healing involves the dynamic interaction between God's working and our wanting. If we know that we need healing in some form, then it is insufficient to assume that we have only to watch and wait for the Lord to respond. We must want to be healed and, with faith and in prayer, we must ask the Lord for that healing. By our cooperation with the Lord we discern the means through which the needed healing will come to us. The Lord can and may take extraordinary measures in accomplishing a healing, but the gift can and may touch us through the simplest and most ordinary, everyday realities. We bear the responsibility of making the efforts necessary to invite the Lord's work of healing into our life.

Healing is the Lord's work; it is offered not imposed. Healing is powerful evidence of the Spirit's presence and activity, but that power does not complete its work by force. God is love and so works by love; all the gifts we receive are expressions and extensions of God's great love for us. If we choose not to acknowledge and accept the gifts, if we are not open to their work within us, God will wait. Free will is among the greatest gifts we have by our creation in God's own image and likeness. God respects and cares for that creation; force is not a part of the plan. Gifts are presented by invitation and even exhortation; it is for us to welcome them.

"Do You Want to Be Made Well?"

This is the question of healing. Its focus is particularly intriguing. Jesus does not ask, "Do you believe that I can heal you?" Rather than focusing on his ability, he appeals to our desire. Do we want to be made well? We may assume that we would give an affirmative response without the slightest hesitation. But when we recognize what needs to be done, we may decide that we are quite comfortable with a less-than-perfect situation. We can discover that, deep within our hearts, we may not want to be healed if we have to confront difficult issues, deal with disrupted relationships, admit our vulnerability, and inevitably make the changes that will be required for healing and wholeness in our life. We can become so accustomed to the attention and sympathy our condition elicits that we prefer and choose not to lose them. We must decide if we want to be healed; we must determine if we want Jesus' presence and activity to make a difference in our life. That decision and determination will mark the quality of our life; they will stand as our response to Jesus' question.

"Could You Not Stay Awake with Me for One Hour?"

Jesus said to the disciples, "I am deeply grieved, even to death; remain here, and stay awake with me." And going a little farther, he threw himself on the ground and prayed, "My Father, if it is possible, let this cup pass from me; yet not what I want but what you want." Then he came to the disciples and found them sleeping; and he said to Peter, "So, could you not stay awake with me for one hour?" (Matthew 26:38-40)

A familiar and festive meal with wine, blessed by prayers and promises ancient and quite new, followed by a walk to a garden on this sultry evening, and now the invitation to stay awake and pray with a friend. When these elements combine with the tension of the last few days, it is not at all surprising that three times Jesus finds his disciples sleeping. It is no wonder that "their eyes were heavy" (26:43).

Jesus' question appears somewhat ill-timed or at least out of place. The celebration and activity immediately preceding this scene in Gethsemane have conspired to create a time and setting in which sleep comes irresistibly. But there is a deeper concern here. Jesus is also asking, "Can you be with me at this difficult time?" This is the moment of Jesus' decision, the time to embrace fully all that God will ask of him in the coming hours. Simply because this is God's will is no assurance that what unfolds will be pleasant or even likable. Quite the contrary. So Jesus prays, "If it is possible, let this cup pass from me; yet not what I want but what you want." It is a time for wanting and needing human companionship; it is an especially difficult and lonely point on the journey.

This is the question of PRAYER. This is the question for maintaining and sustaining our relationship with the Lord through a discipline of prayer that has daily, monthly, yearly components. Possibly we may even have some components that are but once in a lifetime. Jesus' question is not designed to evoke guilt; unfortunately however, it is often used in that way when speaking about the importance of maintaining our spiritual life. His question focuses more on the priorities we establish for our life and whether we recognize our need to be with the Lord, to watch with the Lord, in difficult moments and throughout our everyday life.

As it was noted in the earlier reflections on faith, there are a multitude of prayer forms within the spiritual tradition of the church. The common thread which weaves together all those forms is the simple truth that prayer serves as a means for us to be in relationship with the Lord, as individuals and as a faith community. The quality of our response to Jesus' question will be built upon the principles we use to develop that relationship. A text from Saint Paul's letter to the Romans indicates some basic principles which can shape our personal and communal discipline of prayer.

> The Spirit helps us in our weakness; for we do not know how to pray as we ought, but that very Spirit intercedes with sighs too deep for words. And God, who searches the heart, knows what is the mind of the Spirit, because the Spirit intercedes for the saints according to the will of God. (8:26-27)

In this section of his letter, Saint Paul writes of our life in union with the Spirit through the death and resurrection of Jesus. In this life we wait with great hope for the fulfillment of Jesus' promises. Thus, "the whole of creation has been groaning" (8:22) with anticipation as it waits for the glory which is to come. So too, we groan as we look forward to the "redemption of our bodies" (8:23).

And, as we see in the text above, even the Spirit groans (sighs) on our behalf. Paul creates an image of the entire universe praying with expectation and anticipation. What basic principles can we glean from this rich Pauline text?

Prayer Expresses Our Trust in God

"The Spirit helps us in our weakness." Typical of Saint Paul's writing style, this opening phrase is densely packed. If we are to recognize the Spirit's help as it supports and accompanies us, then we must also acknowledge and accept our need for that assistance. We must recognize that we are weak. We are not completely self-contained, though we may prefer to think that we need very few supportive resources outside ourselves. Prayer begins with a healthy self-knowledge that sees those dimensions of our life which especially need the transforming power of God's grace to move them beyond complacent self-satisfaction. Such complacency constitutes one of the most stubborn stumbling blocks to our continued and consistent growth and development in the spiritual life. Self-knowledge enables us to identify it and urges us to seek the Spirit's help in addressing it.

Self-knowledge is not simply a once-in-a-lifetime exercise for initiating our prayer. It must accompany us throughout our spiritual journey.

However, this does not mean that we remain fixed on exactly the same areas of our life and our relationship with God. As one dimension of life is transformed by God's grace, so other dimensions needing the touch of that grace will come to light. Self-knowledge impels us to respond; it remembers past growth, but that does not complete its task. The importance of self-knowledge within the spiritual life and for our prayer rests upon the reality of the Incarnation. God dwells within us. The journey to union with God, our growth in God-knowledge, is closely associated with our developing self-knowledge, for we journey to God through the self.

Inseparably linked with self-knowledge is humility which admits that "we do not know how to pray as we ought." Humility sees this weakness and so urges us to seek help from the Spirit. Insufficient is any interpretation of this phrase which assumes that Saint Paul has in mind some universal approach to prayer that must be incorporated into the personal and communal spiritual discipline of every Christian. What Paul speaks about here has little or nothing to do with mandatory methods, but everything to do with our deepest desires. This is similar to the disciples' request that Jesus teach them to pray. As Jews, the disciples surely would have been familiar with the basic prayer forms to be practiced by each person and by the synagogue community. They had learned what to do in prayer. But their observation of Jesus' own prayer, his relationship with God, and his teachings about the coming reign of God whets their appetite for more than they had experienced thus far. Their simple request, "Teach us to pray" (Luke 11:1), goes beyond asking for instruction in a new method. They want to pray in a way that touches their deepest desires, that reflects the truth of who they are. This is also our request. In humility we ask for assistance in praying with the desires that are deep within our heart.

Prayer expresses our trust in God, our dependence upon God, our conviction that God is present and active in our life, our confidence that God is ever with us along the pathways of our spiritual journey. If we cannot trust, then it is unlikely that we would sense any need for prayer in our life. Trust is built upon a healthy self-knowledge that is not afraid to confront our need for God, and a sincere humility which does not hesitate in requesting and seeking the support necessary for continued growth and development. Our commitment to prayer reflects the strength of faith which assures us that "the Spirit helps us in our weakness."

Prayer is the Spirit's Voice Within Us

The fact that "we do not know how to pray as we ought" would be quite discouraging if we had to rely solely on our own resources. We might never discover how to pray as we ought. However, we need not pray alone. Our trust in God assures us that "the Spirit helps us in our weakness." This help is much more than a disinterested assistance; "that very Spirit intercedes with sighs too deep for words." The Spirit prays within us and for us. Whether or not we are aware of it or perceive it, we are not completely alone and voiceless when we go before the Lord in prayer. The voice of the Spirit, deep within us, intercedes, praises, thanks, and petitions the Lord on our behalf. This, too, is a gift of the Incarnation, a grace from the Spirit of truth whom Jesus promised would be with us forever. This is the Spirit whom Jesus says "abides with you, and will be in you" (John 14:17). This is the voice that prays within us.

The Spirit's presence and prayer do not exonerate us from the need to establish a personal discipline of prayer. Even with the Spirit's help, our spiritual life remains our own responsibility; we build it and maintain it. The alternative is a complacency which not only slows our progress in the spiritual life, but has the potential to erode it altogether. The specific components for our personal discipline need not follow some standardized recipe. Rather, they should reflect our personality and capability, our daily tasks and activities, precisely so our fidelity to that discipline is truly feasible. Any personal discipline of prayer which cannot be practiced realistically and regularly has little possibility for facilitating and nurturing a genuine transformation within any dimension of our life.

The Spirit's voice within us proclaims the truth of our identity. Saint Paul writes, "the Spirit bears witness with our spirit that we are children of God" (Romans 8:16). The voice of the Spirit praying within us acknowledges and affirms the dignity of our creation in God's own image and likeness. That voice blends with our own, reminding us of that dignity. Such a reminder is crucial in the face of so many societal and cultural forces that tend to undermine our dignity, or to displace it with materials and priorities that are not consistent with the depth and beauty of who and what we truly are as human beings. We can mistake those materials and priorities as necessities required for sustaining our self-worth when, in fact, they draw whatever worth they have from our dignity as humans. The united chorus of the Spirit's voice with our own proclaims that we are "heirs of God and joint heirs with Christ" (Romans 8:17). This proclamation is at the very heart of our prayer, this proclamation is the truth of our identity.

Prayer is the Spirit's voice within us. We can pray with many voices. Our hopes and our hurts, our blessings and our burdens, our graces and our griefs — all these are given a voice through our prayer. All these reflect the reality of our everyday life. And within that reality the Spirit's voice speaks out, to help us, to pray with us and for us, in "sighs too deep for words." Those sighs become a resounding witness of the mystery and majesty of our creation.

Prayer is a Matter of the Heart

Prayer cannot be summed up by our hands, our habits, or our history. It comes from deeper realms; prayer is from the heart. God "searches the heart." It is from there that we build our relationship with the Lord; it is from the heart that we pray. Within our heart the Spirit helps us; from that deep center within us, the Spirit prays with "sighs too deep for words." In this context, the term *heart* refers to our deepest self, our identity, our hopes for the future, and our desires to realize those hopes. God "searches the heart" precisely to touch who we truly are and to sustain the life of the Spirit within us.

A human tendency within the spiritual life is to imagine that prayer is fundamentally an external practice; that is, something we do with our hands and through the routine of our habits. Yet, prayer is more than what we do and even more than the frequency with which we do it. Simply because we pray in a particular way, using a specific method or ritual at regular intervals, is no assurance that our heart is united with our hands and our habits. The Pharisees had their methods and rituals and we know that very often Jesus was less than impressed by their displays for attention (see Matthew 6:1-18; 23:23-30; Luke 11:39). Of course there are very concrete elements in a healthy discipline of personal prayer; our discipline cannot be completely amorphous. The challenge is to assure that our practice does not degenerate into a perfunctory performance with no passion. Passion is rooted in the heart; our hands and our habits in prayer must mirror the truth within our heart.

Prayer is a living reality, it is not meant to be set in stone by our history and then remain untouched forever and ever amen. The spiritual journey is an adventure; it opens us to new panoramas, leads us onto new pathways, and guides us toward new peaks of awareness and learning. Nevertheless, we must choose, we must decide to see those panoramas and enter those pathways and climb those peaks. Assuredly the Lord will be with us, accompanying us along the way; prayer postures us to listen for the Lord's presence and activity in our life. We can allow our history to hasten or hinder our progress, to sharpen or shield our ability to listen for the Lord; the choice is ours. Past experiences and learnings are valuable for our spiritual life. However, if we cling to them so tightly that we close the door to whatever new experiences and learnings may be yet before us, then we compromise our potential for continued growth and development in our prayer, in our spiritual life, and in our relationship with the Lord.

Prayer is a matter of the heart. "God searches the heart" because it is familiar territory, reflecting our creation in God's image and likeness. There is room for God in the heart; its capacity and potential are limitless by nature. God is at home in the heart. However, the constrictions and restrictions we place on it with our fears and doubts and hesitations do affect that nature — at least temporarily — so its capacity will appear much less spacious. Prayer, as a matter of the heart, also has limitless potential. Still, its growth and development can be constricted and restricted through the practices of our hands, the persistence of our habits, and the perspectives from our history. If we do not attend to our heart in the face of all this, then it could gradually harden into an impenetrable monolith with room enough only for itself.

"Could You Not Stay Awake with Me for One Hour?"

This is the question of prayer. We can view this question from two perspectives. First, staying awake and praying and being with the Lord for "one hour" require a dedication of time and energy. The wisdom of this perspective is consistency. Our personal discipline of prayer must take place in real time, with a commitment to spend some period with the Lord, in some way, each day. Whether the "hour" is a full sixty minutes is not as significant as whether our relationship with the Lord is in fact allotted a regular space in our daily schedule. Second, we stay awake and pray and remain with the Lord throughout our life. The wisdom of this perspective is fidelity. The daily "hour" we dedicate to the Lord reflects the quality of relationship we establish and maintain with the Lord. Our prayer thus becomes a mirror of our life, a reflection of the priority we assign to the Lord in our everyday life. Consistency and fidelity are the marks of a healthy discipline of prayer. The question thus awaits our response. "Could you not stay awake with me for one hour?" Can you pray with me, for now and for life?

"Whom Are You Looking For?"

Judas brought a detachment of soldiers together with police from the chief priests and the Pharisees, and they came there with lanterns and torches and weapons. Then Jesus, knowing all that was to happen to him, came forward and asked them, "Whom are you looking for?" They answered, "Jesus of Nazareth." Jesus replied, "I am he."… They stepped back and fell to the ground. Again he asked them, "Whom are you looking for?" (John 18:3-7)

This scene is so well-ordered and smooth-flowing that it could be described as choreographed. One key to understanding the interaction that unfolds here lies in Saint John's characterization of Jesus as "knowing all that was to happen to him." His hour had arrived. Though he is arrested and led away, Jesus is very much in control here. He knows his priorities, he decides, he chooses all that will happen in the next few hours. These events are not thrust upon him as an unwilling and helpless victim. He challenges this mob to state their purpose, to name whom they are looking for.

This scene before his death is not the only occasion on which Jesus asks this question. A second incident occurs three days after his death, near the tomb where he was buried. Mary Magdalene "turned around and saw Jesus standing there, but she did not know that it was Jesus. Jesus said to her, 'Woman, why are you weeping? Whom are you looking for?'" (John 20:14-15). In both instances the respondents must state clearly what they are doing. Jesus' question demands clarity and precision.

This is the question of MOTIVES. It is the question for discerning and discovering what we are doing with our life, why we do what we do, and how our life is unfolding. This is not a once-in-a-lifetime question; rather, it must mark the entirety of our spiritual journey. Even more, in a variety of ways and depending upon the situations we encounter, we may confront this question even on a daily basis. Every time we come to a crossroads, every instance in which clarity is not so evident, this question stands before us. Our response must be alive, marking the decisions we make and the directions we take through our everyday tasks and responsibilities. That response will either confirm or contradict the vitality of our faith, the integrity with which we use our gifts, our consistency in addressing our need for healing, and our fidelity to prayer.

The quality of our response to Jesus' question can be enhanced by our understanding of the role that motives have in our spiritual life. A familiar statement from Jesus in Saint Matthew's gospel provides a useful framework for exploring that understanding.

> Ask, and it will be given you; search, and you will find; knock, and the door will be opened for you. For everyone who asks receives, and everyone who searches finds, and for everyone who knocks, the door will be opened. (7:7-8)

There is a double dynamic at work here, giving this text a special richness. First is the dynamic of action and response: ask-given, search-find, knock-opened; the use of active and passive verbs highlights this dynamic. The point is simple. If we expect a response, then we must act. Second is the dynamic of present and future; the tenses of the verbs highlight this dynamic. Again, the point is plain. What we do now shapes our quality of life for the future. Both these dynamics reflect our intention to nurture the quality of our life, and that intention is brought to life through our motives. What are some principal roles of motives within the spiritual life?

Motives Reveal Values

"Ask, and it will be given you." Whether our request is for general information or specific instructions or some type of assistance and support, it reflects a need we have. Our request is born of a desire for access to something we consider valuable and necessary for our immediate situation and possibly for our entire life. Our motive for making the request reveals the value we have assigned to the response we hope to receive. Precisely because of this connection between our motives and the values on which they are based can we interpret the meaning of why we do what we do. Thus, the meaning in our life can begin to wane if we lose touch with the values that give stability and substance to it. Why we do what we do will then become much less clear, to others and even to ourselves. Our motives and the actions which flow from them will gradually communicate more pretense than principle.

The primary value by which we are called to live as followers of the Lord Jesus is love. Love above all must shape the motives which guide our actions. This truth gives rise to some probing questions. Are we motivated by love? Do we want our everyday life to reflect the teaching and example of Jesus? What steps do we take — specifically — to nurture our growth as loving people? Jesus teaches us — indeed, commands us — to love. He also teaches us some very concrete means of living that love. "In everything do to others as you would have them do to you" (Matthew 7:12). "'Lord, … how often should I forgive? As many as seven times?' Jesus said to him, 'Not seven times, but, I tell you, seventy-seven times'" (Matthew 18:21-22). What motives do our actions reflect? What values do our motives reveal?

Even if our motives remain unarticulated, the values which shape them become visible through our relationships and through our casual encounters with others on a daily basis. Our interactions with others, our treatment of them, our openness to work with them, to assist and support them, our willingness to seek and extend forgiveness — all this speaks of the values by which we choose to live. Our relationships demonstrate the integrity of our intention to live the example and teaching of Jesus. The consequence of that truth is incontrovertible. "Just as you did it to one of the least of these who are members of my family, you did it to me" (Matthew 25:40). And a few moments later Jesus teaches the other side of this truth with equal force. "Just as you did not do it to one of the least of these, you did not do it to me" (25:45). What Jesus did and taught are not theories to be considered at our leisure. They constitute a way of life we must choose by the values we hold and through the motives which guide our actions.

Motives reveal values. Why we do what we do either supports or subverts the integrity of our efforts to live the gospel much more than any proclamation we can make, however eloquent. Actions do indeed speak louder than words. And when those actions are guided by motives which reflect our commitment to live the values of the gospel, then our daily life makes a significant contribution to the continuation of Jesus' mission and message.

Motives Give Direction to Life

"Search, and you will find." We search precisely because we want to find something or we hope to arrive at some point. Of course the quality of what we find will be determined, to some degree, by how seriously and sincerely we take up the search. That search, propelled by our motives, takes us on a journey in a definite direction and, indeed, gives direction to our life. The character and caliber of our motives will set the course for that direction. Apart from our motives we can be left with little if any incentive to search. And without the search, our life can drift along, stripped of both passion and purpose. Motives safeguard us from approaching life as a spectator sport. Life demands our active and decisive participation. The effectiveness of that action and decision will be configured by the motives that mark our spiritual journey. Even at times of confusion and uncertainty, our motives can enable us to articulate — however imprecisely — where we want to be going in life and what we hope to find. Our motives are an important source of energy and excitement on the journey.

Having a direction in life is no guarantee that the pathways we take on our journey will be free of all obstacles. Nor will it guarantee that we are on the best of pathways. Jesus himself alerts us; "Enter through the narrow gate; for the gate is wide and the road is easy that leads to destruction, and there are many who take it. For the gate is narrow and the road is hard that leads to life, and there are few who find it" (Matthew 7:13-14). Our motives can serve as a compass along the way, enabling us to distinguish between the wide and the narrow, between the potential for destruction and the promise of life. Such motives though must be born of faith, enriched by our gifts, and honed through healing and prayer. Such motives will then translate into priorities and practices guiding us on the road "that leads to life."

Our motives configure the decisions we make for our life. Specifically, they indicate where we want to go in life and what we hope to accomplish in life. Our integrity in formulating those motives, our consistency in monitoring them, and our sincerity in adjusting them when necessary so they ever reflect the values we profess, are the true gauges of a quality life. We may discover that the direction which our motives point out to us is not always to our liking. Nevertheless, if those motives have been built and sustained on the values of the gospel, then they will direct us to the Lord. Admittedly, sometimes that will be the Lord of Easter Sunday, surrounding us with the radiance of new life; and sometimes it will be the Lord of Good Friday, inviting us to take a share in the cross. In either case, it is the Lord. The question remains before us. Whom are you looking for? What do you truly desire?

Motives give direction to life. Either they will direct us along pathways taking us ever closer to the Lord or they will draw us into a spiraling selfishness and insularity. At times our actions and motives form a single weaving and so communicate our truest self. At other times our actions may be but a cosmetic display to distract others from seeing the less than pure character and content of our motives. Motives affect the heart for they take root deep within the soil of our very being. If our heart is fixed on the Lord, then our search will be marked as such. If our heart is fixed on something or somewhere else, then that is how and where we will find ourselves when the search is at its end.

As the Lord Jesus has told us, "Where your treasure is, there your heart will be also" (Matthew 6:21).

Motives Are Doors on the Journey

"Knock, and the door will be opened for you." Doors are passageways, points of transition, inviting us into new places and different spaces. The assumption here, of course, is that we want the doors to be opened. Usually, they are so commonplace that they barely catch our attention as we go through the day. Doors become mysterious only when we truly do not know what awaits us on the other side. Then we must decide if indeed we will knock or turn and walk away, allowing the door before us to remain securely closed. Our motives can serve as doors, as points of transition, along the pathways of our spiritual journey. We take particular note of them when we sense changes in our prayer and in the usual routines of our spiritual life. It is for us to determine if we will knock and enter those places and spaces to which our motives will lead us or if we will ignore them, hoping that they will fade away, leaving us contentedly undisturbed.

Motives have a definite impact on our journey. They shape the quality of our growth and development in the spiritual life, for better or for worse. For the better, they become the passageways to continued progress. For the worse, they can be detours that drain our energy and discourage us from making any further efforts in the spiritual life. The difference, of course, lies in what we choose to do and in how we decide to nurture our continuing spiritual growth and development. If we choose and decide to be holy even as the Lord has called us to be holy, then our motives will highlight those actions and attitudes that will facilitate our union with the Lord. If we choose and decide to hesitate, then our motives can imprison us in mediocrity.

Jesus' teaching is blunt. "A good tree cannot bear bad fruit, nor can a bad tree bear good fruit.... Not everyone who says to me, 'Lord, Lord,' will enter the kingdom of heaven, but only the one who does the will of my Father in heaven" (Matthew 7:18, 21). It is not the nature of our motives to lead us into some rarefied world of theories and wishes. They call us to action, they seek the fulfillment of being put into motion. Their value and purpose within our spiritual life lie in their ability to keep us moving along the pathways of the journey. Our motives add vitality and vibrancy to our spiritual life so our progress does not fall victim to procrastination. Jesus' teaching is especially challenging in this regard. It is insufficient only to speak the words, however beautifully formulated they may be. Words must be translated into works. We can spend years articulating what we hope and plan to do without ever making a single effort to realize that hope and plan. The reasons for our delay may be myriad; nevertheless, as long as we choose to delay, our motives will lack any genuinely effective substance.

Motives are doors on the journey. Our passage through those doors, as our continued growth and development in the spiritual life unfold, is propelled by integrity and constancy. The integrity of our motives is confirmed by their congruity with the values which Jesus exemplifies and teaches in the gospel. If our motives do not hinge on those values, then we will open doors and walk along paths that move us further from the Lord or at least that disrupt our progress. Our constancy is confirmed as we actively incorporate those gospel values into the decisions we make and the directions we take every day. If our motives are not steered by those values, then our movement in the spiritual life will be unnecessarily circuitous. We will expend valuable time and energy and yet establish no distinct connection with the direction in which the Lord awaits us.

"Whom Are You Looking For?"

This is the question of motives. Our response to Jesus' question must reflect a longing for God, even a hunger that God be and remain an intimate part of our life. Our motives, and especially what we decide and do in light of those motives, will demonstrate or deny the sincerity of our desire for union with God. Motives are doors which invite us to enter into the life of the Lord, to continue the journey, and to pursue our longing for God. To the degree that our motives lead us to live the values inherent in Jesus' example and teaching, to that degree do we gradually become what we value. We are thus transformed into the living likeness of the Lord. We answer Jesus' question by believing that our life is destined for union with the Lord, we answer Jesus' question by living what we believe.

"Was it Not Necessary?"

Two disciples were going to a village called Emmaus, about seven miles from Jerusalem, and talking with each other about all these things that had happened. While they were talking and discussing, Jesus himself came near and went with them, but their eyes were kept from recognizing him. And he said to them, "What are you discussing with each other while you walk along?" They stood still, looking sad. Then one of them, whose name was Cleopas, answered him, "Are you the only stranger in Jerusalem who does not know the things that have taken place there in these days?" "What things?" They replied, "The things about Jesus of Nazareth, who was a prophet mighty in deed and word before God and all the people, and how our chief priests and leaders handed him over to be condemned to death and crucified him. But we had hoped that he was the one to redeem Israel. Yes, and besides all this, it is now the third day since these things took place. Moreover, some women of our group astounded us. They were at the tomb early this morning, and when they did not find his body there, they came back and told us that they had indeed seen a vision of angels who said that he was alive. Some of those who were with us went to the tomb and found it just as the women had said; but they did not see him." Then he said to them, "Oh, how foolish you are, and how slow of heart to believe all that the prophets have declared! Was it not necessary that the Messiah should suffer these things and then enter into his glory?" (Luke 24:13-26)

This scene demonstrates so well that the cross has been a stumbling block from the very beginnings of Christianity. The hopes of these two disciples, and of many others at the time, were tightly linked to an image of Jesus' triumphant victory over the social, political, and economic forces which held Israel captive. Those hopes had long been refashioned into precise expectations regarding how the Messiah would achieve that triumph.

And those expectations were intertwined with assumptions about the political prowess and the military power needed to assure victory. Just prior to the Ascension, after all the disciples had experienced with Jesus, even then they ask, "Lord, is this the time when you will restore the kingdom to Israel?" (Acts 1:6). They would have preferred to lay aside any remembrance of those unpleasant events that immediately preceded the Resurrection. Those expectations and assumptions could be blinding and surely contributed to the reason that the disciples "were kept from recognizing him."

In his encounter with the disciples on the road to Emmaus, Jesus bluntly addresses those expectations and assumptions. Quite simply, they are foolish. They have little if anything to do with the ways that God has chosen to work among the people. Those ways have been made clear in God's word; they were evident in "all that the prophets have declared!" What Jesus suffered, then, however unpleasant for his followers, was not really a surprise in terms of all that God had said to the people throughout salvation history. In fact, as Jesus asks, "Was it not necessary?"

This is the question of the CROSS. It is the question for exploring the meaning and the role of the cross in our life. There are many ways to describe the crosses we experience in life, depending upon their type and timing. "Necessary," however, may not be among the first descriptive words that come to mind. And yet that is how Jesus characterizes his own cross. If we desire to follow the example established by the Lord Jesus, then can we expect anything less?

Our response to Jesus' question can mark the difference between tapping the power for transformation within the crosses we experience and missing the graced opportunities for growing in our likeness to the Lord. What can be said of the necessity of the cross? In speaking of the requirements for following him, Jesus gives a prominent place to the cross.

> If any want to become my followers, let them deny themselves and take up their cross and follow me. For those who want to save their life will lose it, and those who lose their life for my sake will find it. (Matthew 16:24-25)

What can be said about this cross that must be taken up? What can we know about this cross that is intimately linked to life? Why is it necessary?

The Cross is Inevitable

Jesus instructs us to "take up" the cross. The assumption here is that the cross will be readily at hand, well within our reach. Experiencing the cross is inevitable in our life. It does not present itself as an option for us to consider at our leisure. It can and will come in many forms, emerging within any dimension of our life — physical, emotional, psychological, relational, spiritual. If we are alive, the cross will come. The only point we need to consider is whether we will take it up or pretend to ignore it. The latter approach will consume a great deal of time and energy without contributing to our growth and development toward union with God. Gradually, we learn that taking up the cross is inseparable from following Jesus.

It is intriguing to note that Jesus does not instruct us to search for the cross. The very fact that the cross is inevitable, and thus accessible, would preclude the need for any extensive search. But there is a more significant point here that touches the quality of our growth and development in the spiritual life. If we search for the cross, then we risk creating and customizing it according to our own preference and convenience so it does not disrupt our scheduled plans. Self-created crosses are truly expressions of pride regardless of how weighty we construct them to appear. Ultimately, they are decorative and designed to shine the spotlight on us, to draw attention to ourselves. The crosses which come to us, not of our own making, challenge us to remain focused and fixed on the Lord. The inevitability of the cross means that we cannot control its nature or its nuances. The cross is for taking up; making it up has little connection with Jesus' invitation to those who would follow him.

Within that invitation, Jesus instructs his followers to take up "their cross." The cross is personal, it is not exactly the same for every individual. Even when there are parallels in the experiences of the cross shared by two or more people, each person will react and respond according to individual personality, perceptions, and priorities. Though the external reality of their crosses may appear to be quite similar, their personal experiences and interpretations can be at the opposite ends of a spectrum. The cross ever remains uniquely and intimately their own as individuals.

The cross is inevitable, and it is personal. This, however, does not cancel the potential we have for supporting and accompanying others in their experiences of the cross. This does not diminish the need for compassion. Rather, it is a reminder that we cannot take away the cross of another person. We can comfort and encourage and assist, but the experience is truly their own. Our presence and concern are valuable gifts we can share; we have the responsibility to offer them. But they are not erasers, they will not make the cross go away. The cross must be taken up, inevitably and personally. This is what Jesus has called us to do.

The Cross Marks the Way of Jesus

The conditional phrase with which Jesus opens his instruction is revealing, "If any want to become my followers." We must want — desire and choose — to follow Jesus if his teaching is to have any relevance for us and any influence in our life. If Jesus is not the root of our faith, the source of our gifts, our hope of healing, the center of our prayer, and the goal of our motives, then we can lay aside this instruction and let others tend to it. If we do want to follow Jesus, then we must embrace the threefold discipline he articulates for us: renouncing self, accepting the cross, and living his example. These three mark the way to union with Jesus.

Self-renunciation is, essentially, a simple reality. It is a means by which we make room for God. Our life can become cluttered with so much internal and external stuff that there is very little breathing space for anything or anyone else, including God. One aspect of self-renunciation involves clearing a space in our life so that God's place is assured some priority. Maintaining that space may require some rearrangement of our values. Saint Paul expresses it well; "I regard everything as loss because of the surpassing value of knowing Christ Jesus my Lord. For his sake I have suffered the loss of all things, and I regard them as rubbish, in order that I may gain Christ and be found in him" (Philippians 3:8-9). Simply clearing a space within and around ourselves is no guarantee that we will allow God to fill that space. We must, in fact, establish our relationship with the Lord Jesus as the highest priority in our life. Then, we must do whatever is necessary to maintain that priority.

The process and effort involved in that rearrangement of values are significant parts of taking up our cross. Following the Lord as the highest priority in our life will cost us something. It can cost us our life; that is, our identity as we have constructed it. Following Jesus requires that we find our true identity in union with the Lord. It is for such union that we were created. Whatever could hinder our journey toward that union — possessions or practices or perspectives — must be displaced by our relationship with the Lord. That displacement is the cross we must embrace, it is the cost we must bear. Taking up the cross and accepting the cost constitute our following of the Lord; they are the foundations for living as Jesus lived.

The cross marks the way of Jesus. There is no other way. It would be convenient and, no doubt, more to our liking if the story were such that we could proceed directly from the festive meal of Holy Thursday to the glory and joy of Easter Sunday. But as it is, we must pass by way of Good Friday. Living as Jesus lived confronts us with the stark reality of our own cross. It remains for us to decide how we will respond to that confrontation. We can embrace the cross and so trace the pathways that Jesus walked toward union with God. Or, we can run from the cross, pretend it is not before us, and so travel the road to an uncertain destination in our spiritual life. The choice is ours.

The Cross is the Means to Life

"Those who want to save their life will lose it, and those who lose their life for my sake will find it." The cross is about life, new life, quality life. Without the perspective of faith, this statement from Jesus makes no sense at all. We cherish life, we seek to preserve life, and yet Jesus presents this paradox which will remain confusing and unsettling if accorded only a cursory reading. Examined with faith, however, Jesus' words make perfect sense. If we construct our own life, solidify our own identity, with no considerations or influences other than those we personally scrutinize and select, then we jeopardize a genuine openness to God's work in our life. We can become insensitive to God's loving presence and activity within and around us. Without that openness, we can lose touch with the quality of life which reflects our creation in God's image and likeness.

Wanting to save our own life, from the gospel perspective, involves much more than prudent and responsible physical self-care. It reaches even to our spiritual life and to our very identity as creatures of a loving God. Whether or not we articulate it as such, we become a self-savior by recreating ourselves according to an image and likeness that suit own our preferences and priorities. We may indeed "save" the life we have constructed, but we can lose the life to which God calls us. At the very least, we will diminish our ability to hear and respond to that call. However sophisticated and comprehensive our design for life, it will eventually fall short of what God desires for us. As Saint Paul reminds us, "no eye has seen, nor ear heard, nor the human heart conceived, what God has prepared for those who love him" (1 Corinthians 2:9).

Only in the cross will we find the life promised to us and prepared for us. Losing our life, from the gospel perspective, enables us to be sufficiently vulnerable for God's life to take root and to develop within us. We willingly lay aside our blueprint for self-recreation precisely so God can work deeply within our heart and gradually transform us into the Lord's own likeness. This willing loss of life, of control over the design of our life, is not random. Its guiding motive is clear. It is done "for my sake," for the Lord, to live as the Lord lived, to love as the Lord loves, to follow the Lord. The life which the cross brings to us comes by God's grace and through our willingness and efforts to be like the Lord in all things.

The cross is the means to life. It may not be the most popular or pleasant means we could imagine; nevertheless, it has been established by the Lord Jesus as the path to life, to resurrection, to union with God. The challenge for us is to believe, with Saint Paul, that "the sufferings of this present time are not worth comparing with the glory about to be revealed to us" (Romans 8:18). Such faith will not make our immediate experience of the cross any less weighty or painful, but it can remind us that there is life behind the cross, that the radiance of Easter Sunday will shine even though all we can see at the moment is the darkness of Good Friday. Truly, there is a "glory about to be revealed to us," but it is a glory that comes by journeying along the passageways of the cross.

"Was it Not Necessary?"

This is the question of the cross. Whatever may be our experiences of the cross, whichever dimensions of life it may touch, our response to Jesus' question will reflect whether we will take up the cross as a blessing that holds the promise of new life, or attempt to avoid it as an unnecessary burden that brings nothing but pain. We cannot control the type or timing of the crosses we will encounter in life. Only our faith in the Lord and our love for the Lord will enable us to confront those crosses as necessary for our spiritual life. Often we can see that necessity with the grace of hindsight, as we identify and celebrate the ways in which we have grown and developed through our past experiences of the cross. The alternative is to be consumed by a persistent bitterness or anger which has little to do with the life that Jesus promises to those who follow him. The cross is about life. The cross is about embracing fully the example of Jesus. And living that example is necessary if we want to be one with the Lord.

"Do You Love Me?"

Jesus said to Simon Peter, "Simon son of John, do you love me more than these?" He said to him, "Yes, Lord; you know that I love you." Jesus said to him, "Feed my lambs." A second time Jesus said to him, "Simon son of John, do you love me?" He said to him, "Yes, Lord; you know that I love you." Jesus said, "Tend my sheep." He said to him the third time, "Simon son of John, do you love me?" (John 21:15-17)

In the gospels, Saint Peter often presents himself as bold, even brash, self-assured, confident and convinced he was doing the right thing at the right time. Until this scene with Jesus on the shore after breakfast, Peter may have simply assumed that Jesus would know of his love. Of course, the question had never been asked this directly. Now it has been asked, and more than once. The gospel itself notes that this was an unsettling encounter for

Peter. He was "hurt because he said to him the third time, 'Do you love me?'" (John 21:17). His final response is not built upon any eloquent explanations. He points to the truth that he believes is shared between Jesus and himself, "Lord, you know everything; you know that I love you" (*ibid.*).

This is the question of LOVE. It is the question for determining not only the quality of our relationship with the Lord, but the caliber of our relationships with all people. It is the question for deciding if we take seriously the example and teaching of Jesus. It accompanies us all the time, and most especially in our encounters with family, friends, and co-workers. Our response to this particular question reflects the sincerity of our responses to Jesus' questions of faith, gifts, healing, prayer, motives, and the cross. However refined those responses may be, if they do not lead us to love, then they are not truly a part of what we claim to desire for our spiritual journey.

Of all Jesus' teachings, one in particular summarizes the entirety of the word that he preached and the work that he did among the people.

> I give you a new commandment, that you love one another. Just as I have loved you, you also should love one another. By this everyone will know that you are my disciples, if you have love for one another. (John 13:34-35)

This teaching is clear and uncompromising. It articulates the basic perspective and practice that Jesus established for his followers. He situates himself at the very heart of that perspective and practice as essential to the continuation of his mission and message. This "new commandment" encompasses the whole of Christian life. What are the fundamental insights that Jesus presents in this teaching?

Love is the Mandate

"I give you a new commandment, that you love one another." Initially, the disciples must have been somewhat surprised to hear that they were to receive yet another commandment. They were already familiar with the law as it had been given to Moses at Mount Sinai. In addition, by this time, the scribes and Pharisees had generated extensive and detailed legal regulations to cover every aspect of daily life. In fact, there were more than six hundred such regulations to which the Jewish community was expected to be attentive. Jesus gives this new commandment in the context of a sacred meal, not long before his arrest and execution. Much more than another piece of legal minutiae, this commandment summarizes everything Jesus has done and taught during his private life and his public ministry.

With this commandment, Jesus sets the standard and establishes the mandate for all of Christian life. Love is the path along which we follow Jesus and the practice by which we live and minister as Jesus lived and ministered. All the other virtues and qualities which mark Jesus' presence and activity among the people are radiant reflections of his love. It must be the same for us. Love must mark our life and work; it is the criterion for determining the effectiveness of our efforts to follow Jesus. It provides the pattern by which we will "grow up in every way into him who is the head, into Christ" (Ephesians 4:15).

Love is a simple mandate, but we know it can be hard work. It cannot exist on the theoretical level, love must be realized in our relationships with others. Here is the principal challenge — dealing with other people on a daily basis. If our love is not visible and vibrant in our everyday relationships — with all their ups and downs — then it is not real. It is reduced to lofty words with little weight. The love which Jesus commands of his followers is practical and pervasive. It is at work all the time and in every situation. By its nature, love does not limit itself with restrictions based on the difficulty of the situation or relationship at hand. We manufacture and maintain such restrictions because we perceive that the difficulty is beyond our ability, or we choose not to become further involved in the situation or relationship so we can avoid the inconvenience.

Love is the mandate. Love encompasses the entirety of our spiritual journey, it summarizes the whole process of our transformation into the likeness of Jesus. We can approach our spiritual life as a multitude of rituals and practices which must be scrupulously observed. Such an approach brings with it the very real possibility that we could neglect "the weightier matters of the law: justice and mercy and faith" (Matthew 23:23). And love. The pathways of our journey may be circuitous at times, the process of our transformation may be tedious, but our fidelity in striving to live and minister as Jesus lived and ministered will gradually fashion us into people of love, people of the Lord. That is the very ground and goal of the spiritual journey.

Love is the Mission

"Just as I have loved you, you also should love one another." The commandment to love others had long been established by the time Jesus speaks these words. Centuries earlier, in the book of Leviticus, it had been written, "Love your neighbor as yourself" (19:18). Yet Jesus describes the commandment he gives to the disciples as "new." Its distinctiveness lies in the standard which Jesus now establishes: "as I have loved you." Jesus' example becomes the standard for love as it is the standard for Christian life. Any and all other standards are secondary to the pattern of love evident in Jesus' life, death, resurrection, and continuing presence and activity among us.

By using the standard of his own example, Jesus provides stability to the reference point for love. Loving others "as yourself" has as many variations as there are individuals. The caliber and extent of love can shift from person to person depending upon past experiences, perspectives, preferences, personality, and a plethora of other factors unique to each individual. And what of those who struggle to love themselves or who do not love themselves because of their personal history and present experience? How will they live the standard to "love your neighbor as yourself"? This multitude of variations in the standard for love can diminish our understanding of Jesus' mandate and mission. Ultimately, it can diminish our understanding of the Incarnation.

The mission that Jesus entrusted to us is love. It will be overwhelming if we envision Jesus' example as a series of tasks to be accomplished. We see Jesus preaching and teaching, healing and casting out demons, debating the authorities and discussing theology with those who want to know about him. If our approach is to mimic Jesus, attempting to repeat his actions, then we will be quickly exhausted and discouraged with our failure to match such a multifaceted standard of life.

Jesus teaches us, "my yoke is easy, and my burden is light" (Matthew 11:30). Love is the yoke and the burden. Love is the standard. If we want to live the example of Jesus, then we need only love, for this is to accomplish all that he taught and did.

Love is the mission. The people of Jesus' time were often amazed at him because "he taught them as one having authority, and not as their scribes" (Matthew 7:29). That authority was based on the truth of God's word which Jesus taught and in the integrity with which he lived that word. There was an inseparable bond between his words and his works. What he taught, he did. He preached compassion and forgiveness and love, he was compassionate and forgiving and loving. This is the mission before us, to live and love as Jesus lived and loved. In that mission we will reflect Jesus in our words and our works; by that mission we will be marked as people of love; and through that mission we will continue Jesus' own loving presence and activity in the world today.

Love is the Message

"By this everyone will know that you are my disciples, if you have love for one another." Love is the mandate from Jesus, love is the mission of Jesus; love, then, must be what and how we communicate about Jesus. The mode of communication that Jesus establishes is particularly intriguing. Our love for one another will be the most eloquent testimony we can give of Jesus' life and teaching. Love is the principal means we have for proclaiming the gospel, for love is the language of the gospel. It is a universal language that adapts to every culture and every situation. As a language, love needs few words; its alphabet is constituted by the quality of our relationships and interactions with others.

Love is at the very foundation of Christian identity. We will be known as followers of Jesus by our love for one another. This raises the question, what will we be known as if we do not love one another? While Jesus does not respond to this directly, we can infer an important truth from what he does tell us. If love is the main means through which we communicate the word and work of Jesus to others, then apart from love, we are silent regardless of our volume level. Quite simply, we will not be heard. Even more, we will not be seen, at least not as followers of Jesus. If we translate Jesus' teaching into the negative, his message is equally haunting — if we do not love one another, then no one will know that we are his disciples. We become invisible. As Saint John instructs us, "let us love, not in word or speech, but in truth and action" (1 John 3:18).

Love is no romantic nicety. It is a powerful force by which our world desperately needs to be touched. As followers of Jesus, we bear the responsibility of cooperating with God's grace in the work of transforming this world through love. That is the most significant contribution we can make to building the reign of God. There are serious consequences if we neglect to love. Without the living witness of Jesus' life and teaching that Christians are called to be, our world could quickly believe that generous and selfless love is beyond the range of human potential. Compassion then becomes a commodity that is much too costly — personally, socially, and internationally. It is relegated to a museum of ancient artifacts whose usefulness has long expired. Love and its attendant qualities come to be viewed as theoretical ideals without the practical content for actually getting anything accomplished in this world. Jesus' mandate and mission would gradually fade from the category of those means to be seriously considered as effective for achieving and assuring world peace and justice and unity.

Love is the message. We can claim to be followers of Jesus and to continue his word and his work, but love alone is the measure for determining the integrity of that claim. Without love, our words are wasted and our work is weak. Saint Paul articulates this most eloquently.

> If I speak in the tongues of mortals and
> of angels, but do not have love, I am a

noisy gong or a clanging cymbal. And if I have prophetic powers, and understand all mysteries and all knowledge, and if I have all faith, so as to remove mountains, but do not have love, I am nothing. If I give away all my possessions, and if I hand over my body so that I may boast, but do not have love, I gain nothing. (1 Corinthians 13:1-3)

If we do not strive to love, then we forfeit our effectiveness for continuing and communicating the mandate and the mission of Jesus.

"Do You Love Me?"

There is a story about Saint Francis of Assisi instructing his followers as he prepared them to depart for various places and pursuits. After exhorting them to simplicity of life and union with one another, he told them to proclaim the gospel at all times, in every circumstance and, when necessary, to use words. People should be able to see our proclamation long before they hear it. Our response to Jesus' question must be more than words. It must be evident in all that we do, in our everyday tasks and responsibilities, and most especially in our personal and professional relationships. Love is a verb, it is visible and tangible only when it is put into action. If there is a wide gap between our proclamation of love for the Lord and the caliber of our love for others, then our claim of love for God is little more than lip-service. Jesus has taught us precisely this truth; "just as you did not do it to one of the least of these, you did not do it to me" (Matthew 25:45). Our love for the Lord and our love for others cannot be separated. By love we are transformed into the living likeness of Jesus, by love we carry out the mandate, continue the mission, and communicate the message of Jesus. With Saint Paul, let us pray, "May the Lord make you increase and abound in love for one another and for all" (1 Thessalonians 3:12).

"I Have Something
to Say to You"

The scene from Saint Luke's gospel is well known.
Jesus had been invited to dine in the home of a
Pharisee. A woman, "who was a sinner," ap-
proaches him, bathes his feet with her tears and
dries them with her hair. "Then she continued
kissing his feet and anointing them with the oint-
ment" (7:38). Though the gospel recounts only a
comment from the host, there must have been
much whispering and raising of eyebrows about
Jesus in this socially awkward situation. It was assumed that he "would have known who and what
kind of woman this is who is touching him" (7:39).
Jesus then speaks directly to his host, "'Simon, I
have something to say to you.' 'Teacher,' he replied,
'speak'" (7:40). It is a moment for attention and
anticipation.

Many more are the questions that could be
added to the seven which have been the principal
focus of this work. The questions in this final chap-
ter are a further sampling of those associated with
Jesus that can be used to sharpen our attention and

heighten our anticipation as we continue along the paths of our spiritual journey. Attention and anticipation nurture our growth and development in the spiritual life; they posture us to listen for and respond to the Lord's word. Attention reinforces the priority we give to our relationship with the Lord; anticipation urges us to explore fully the Lord's presence and activity in our daily life. Questions are very much a part of this adventure known as the spiritual journey. They are provisions for that journey.

As we pray with these questions, or others from the gospels, and look with attention and anticipation at where they lead us, we do not need to consider many questions at once. A single question may provide us with more than sufficient material for our prayer time. The key will be to determine which question is the best for us, given the immediate situation in our life. Also, we can decide which form of prayer will be the most effective for us in exploring a particular question.

There are a variety of forms at our disposal. Journaling offers us a forum to explore how the question touches us and what our response calls us to do. We could write a story or a poem about our presence and involvement in a relationship or situation in which the question emerges. Reflective and imaginative forms of meditation are yet another means for allowing the question to shed some light on our immediate life experience. We can envision ourselves as the person responding to the question or as the person asking it. A question or a part of a question could be used as a mantra or a focal point for centering or other types of quiet prayer. Our prayer with the question may simply be a vocal response, in word or song, which intensifies our awareness of the Lord's word and work in our life. Our response to a particular question may find expression through one of the arts. These questions can serve also as a starting point for sharing our prayer and faith within a group.

The form of prayer that we use and our attentiveness to technique must never displace the priority of nurturing our relationship with the Lord and of maintaining a privileged place for the Lord in every dimension of our daily life. That priority is the very purpose of our spiritual life. That priority shapes our faith, supports our gifts, opens us to the Lord's healing, nourishes our prayer, clarifies our motives, enables us to embrace the cross, and builds us up in love.

The following questions are divided into three sections: those from Jesus, those addressed to Jesus, and those asked about Jesus. They are subdivided according to the gospel in which they appear. These questions are presented, purposely, apart from their contexts in the gospels precisely so we can bring them into the context of our personal, everyday life.

Let us pray, then, with attention and antici-

pation as we continue our spiritual journey, trust-
ing that Jesus is ever close to us, always present and
active, ready to guide and encourage, listen and
forgive, nurture and love. We can bring a multitude of concerns and questions to our encounters
with the Lord in prayer and in everyday life. However we must be ever alert, for in those encounters, even before we speak, the Lord Jesus may
speak to us, "I have something to say to you.… I
will also ask you a question" (Luke 7:40; 20:3).
Speak, Lord.

QUESTIONS FROM JESUS

Saint Matthew's Gospel

"If you love those who love you, what reward do
·you have? Do not even the tax collectors do the
same? And if you greet only your brothers and sisters, what more are you doing than others? Do not
even the Gentiles do the same?" (5:46-47)

"Is not life more than food, and the body more
than clothing?… Look at the birds.… Are you not
of more value than they? And can any of you by
worrying add a single hour to your span of life?
And why do you worry about clothing?… If God
so clothes the grass of the field, which is alive today and tomorrow is thrown into the oven, will he

not much more clothe you — you of little faith?" (6:25-30)

"Why do you see the speck in your neighbor's eye, but do not notice the log in your own eye? Or how can you say to your neighbor, 'Let me take the speck out of your eye,' while the log is in your own eye?" (7:3-4)

"Why are you afraid, you of little faith?" (8:26)

"What will it profit them if they gain the whole world but forfeit their life? Or what will they give in return for their life?" (16:26)

"Why do you ask me about what is good?" (19:17)

"What do you think? A man had two sons; he went to the first and said, 'Son, go and work in the vineyard today.' He answered, 'I will not'; but later he changed his mind and went. The father went to the second and said the same; and he answered, 'I go, sir'; but he did not go. Which of the two did the will of his father?" (21:28-31)

Saint Mark's Gospel

"Who are my mother and my brothers?" (3:33)

"Why does this generation ask for a sign?" (8:12)

"Can you see anything?" (8:23)

"What are you arguing about with them?" (9:16)

"Are you able to drink the cup that I drink, or be baptized with the baptism that I am baptized with?" (10:38)

"Why are you putting me to the test?" (12:15)

"My God, my God, why have you forsaken me?" (15:34)

Saint Luke's Gospel

"Why were you searching for me? Did you not know that I must be in my Father's house?" (2:49)

"If you love those who love you, what credit is that to you? … If you do good to those who do good to you, what credit is that to you? … If you lend to those from whom you hope to receive, what credit is that to you?" (6:32-34)

"Can a blind person guide a blind person? Will not both fall into a pit?" (6:39)

"Why do you call me 'Lord, Lord,' and do not do what I tell you?" (6:46)

"Where is your faith?" (8:25)

"What is your name?" (8:30)

"Who touched me?" (8:45)

"Can any of you by worrying add a single hour to your span of life? If then you are not able to do so small a thing as that, why do you worry about the rest?" (12:25-26)

"Do you think that I have come to bring peace to the earth?" (12:51)

"You know how to interpret the appearance of earth and sky, but why do you not know how to interpret the present time?... And why do you not judge for yourselves what is right?" (12:56-57)

"Which of you, intending to build a tower, does not first sit down and estimate the cost, to see whether he has enough to complete it?... Or what king, going out to wage war against another king, will not sit down first and consider whether he is able with ten thousand to oppose the one who comes against him with twenty thousand?" (14:28, 31)

"If then you have not been faithful with dishonest wealth, who will entrust to you true riches? And if you have not been faithful with what belongs to another, who will give you what is your own?" (16:11-12)

"Will not God grant justice to his chosen ones who cry to him day and night? Will he delay long in helping them?" (18:7-8)

"Why are you frightened, and why do doubts arise in your hearts?" (24:38)

Saint John's Gospel

"What are you looking for?" (1:38)

"How can you believe when you accept glory from one another and do not seek the glory that comes from the one who alone is God? ... If you do not believe what (Moses) wrote, how will you believe what I say?" (5:44, 47)

"Why do you not understand what I say?" (8:43)

"Did I not tell you that if you believed, you would see the glory of God?" (11:40)

"Will you lay down your life for me?" (13:38)

"In my Father's house there are many dwelling places. If it were not so, would I have told you that I go to prepare a place for you?" (14:2)

"Do you ask this on your own, or did others tell you about me?" (18:34)

"Have you believed because you have seen me?" (20:29)

QUESTIONS TO JESUS

Saint Matthew's Gospel

"Are you the one who is to come, or are we to wait for another?" (11:3)

"Who is the greatest in the kingdom of heaven?" (18:1)

"Lord, if another member of the church sins against me, how often should I forgive? As many as seven times?" (18:21)

"Teacher, what good deed must I do to have eternal life?… What do I still lack?" (19:16, 20)

"Who can be saved?" (19:25)

"We have left everything and followed you. What then will we have?" (19:27)

"Teacher, which commandment in the law is the greatest?" (22:36)

"Lord, when was it that we saw you hungry and gave you food, or thirsty and gave you something to drink? And when was it that we saw you a stranger and welcomed you, or naked and gave you clothing? And when was it that we saw you sick or in prison and visited you? … Lord, when was it that we saw you hungry or thirsty or a stranger or naked or sick or in prison, and did not take care of you?" (25:37-39, 44)

Saint Mark's Gospel

"By what authority are you doing these things?" (11:28)

"Which commandment is the first of all?" (12:28)

Saint Luke's Gospel

"Who is my neighbor?" (10:29)

"Lord, will only a few be saved?" (13:23)

"Are you, then, the Son of God?" (22:70)

"Are you not the Messiah?" (23:39)

Saint John's Gospel

"Rabbi, where are you staying?" (1:38)

"Where did you get to know me?" (1:48)

"How can these things be?" (3:9)

"What must we do to perform the works of God?" (6:28)

"What sign are you going to give us then, so that we may see it and believe you? What work are you performing?" (6:30)

"Lord, to whom can we go?" (6:68)

"Who are you?" (8:25)

"Surely we are not blind, are we?" (9:40)

"How long will you keep us in suspense?" (10:24)

"Lord, where are you going? Lord, why can I not follow you now?" (13:36, 37)

"What is truth?" (18:38)

QUESTIONS ABOUT JESUS

Saint Matthew's Gospel

"What sort of man is this, that even the winds and the sea obey him?" (8:27)

"Who is this?" (21:10)

Saint Mark's Gospel

"Why does this fellow speak in this way? ... Who can forgive sins but God alone?" (2:7)

"Where did this man get all this? What is this wisdom that has been given to him? ... Is not this the carpenter, the son of Mary and brother of James and Joses and Judas and Simon, and are not his sisters here with us?" (6:2, 3)

Saint Luke's Gospel

"Is not this Joseph's son?" (4:22)

"Why do you look for the living among the dead?" (24:5)

Saint John's Gospel

"He cannot be the Messiah, can he?" (4:29)

"How can this man give us his flesh to eat?" (6:52)

ST PAULS

This book was produced by St. Pauls/Alba House, the Society of St. Paul, an international religious congregation of priests and brothers dedicated to serving the Church through the communications media.

For information regarding this and associated ministries of the Pauline Family of Congregations, write to the Vocation Director, Society of St. Paul, P.O. Box 189, 9531 Akron-Canfield Road, Canfield, Ohio 44406-0189. Phone (330) 702-0359; or E-mail: spvocationoffice@aol.com or check our internet site, www.albahouse.org